I LOVE
LIAM

Are you his ultimate fan?

Written by Jim Maloney

Edited by Philippa Wingate
With thanks to Jonny Marx
Design by Barbara Ward
Cover design by Zoe Bradley

Picture Acknowledgements:
Front and back cover: Dave J Hogan/Getty Images

Picture section:
Page 1, Startraks Photo/Rex Features
Page 2, Rex Features
Page 3, Brian Rasic/Rex Features
Page 4, Brian Rasic/Rex Features
Page 5, Owen Sweeney/Rex Features
Pages 6–7, Ian West/PA Wire/Press Association Images
Page 8, Juan Naharro Gimenez/Getty Images

First published in Great Britain in 2013 by Buster Books,
an imprint of Michael O'Mara Books Limited, 9 Lion Yard, Tremadoc Road,
London SW4 7NQ

www.busterbooks.co.uk

A CIP catalogue record for this book is available from the British Library.

ISBN: 978-1-78055-217-0

10 9 8 7 6 5 4 3 2 1

Printed and bound in February 2013 by CPI Group (UK) Ltd, 108 Beddington Lane,
Croydon, CR0 4YY, United Kingdom.

Papers used by Buster Books are natural, recyclable products made from wood
grown in sustainable forests. The manufacturingprocesses conform to the
environmental regulations of the country of origin.

I LOVE
LIAM

Are you his ultimate fan?

Buster Books

Contents

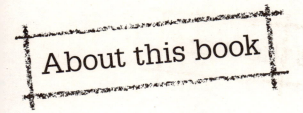

About this book

You love Liam. It's as simple as that.

You watch out for him in every video, follow him on Twitter, and plaster his picture on your bedroom walls. You're definitely a fan. But are you a super fan?

Test your knowledge of all things Liam by taking the cool quizzes and solving the perplexing puzzles in this book. Let your imagination run wild with incredible stories and interviews to fill in. How would you spend your perfect day with Mr Payne?

Grab a pen and follow the instructions at the top of each page. The answers are in the back of the book.

It's brilLiam!

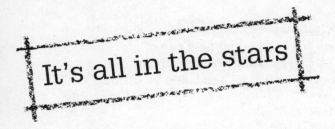

It's all in the stars

YOUR HOROSCOPE CAN REVEAL LOTS ABOUT YOU.
LOOK UP YOUR STAR SIGN AND READ ALL ABOUT WHICH
ROLE IN LIAM'S LIFE WOULD SUIT YOU BEST.

★ **ARIES (21st March – 20th April)** ★
You are a born leader, courageous, enthusiastic and
energetic, with an amazing ability to stay optimistic. You
could be Liam's:

Personal trainer
Your energy and enthusiasm, mixed with an infectious
sense of fun, make you the ideal person to put Liam
through his paces while keeping a smile on his face.

★ **TAURUS (21st April – 21st May)** ★
Dependable, loyal and hard-working, you have excellent
planning skills that always keep you one step ahead. You
could be Liam's:

Housekeeper
Liam trusts you to look after his sanctuary, and you hold
the keys to his castle. It's your job to look after his house,
whether he's home or away – from making sure it stays
squeaky clean to paying the bills.

GEMINI (22nd May – 21st June)

You're always on the look-out for new experiences and the chance to learn new things. You're adaptable and imaginative in every situation. You could be Liam's:

Personal assistant

The sky's the limit when it comes to your loyalty to Liam and, as his personal assistant, you would go to the ends of the Earth for him. He can be confident that you will do everything with energy and enthusiasm.

CANCER (22nd June – 23rd July)

Beneath your sometimes hard shell is a soft marshmallow heart. You are fiercely loyal, and love making a fuss of others. But sometimes you need reassurance. You could be Liam's:

Personal chef

As the lovely Liam's luxury chef, you'd receive the reassurance you need, lapping up his praise when he scoffs down the fancy food you make him and raves about your mouth-watering menus.

⭐ LEO (24th July – 23rd August) ⭐

You are a leader and a trendsetter, both charismatic and optimistic, bold and lively. You have a real passion for life. You could be Liam's:

Costume designer

Your flair and confidence are just what Liam needs to give him an individual look on stage that suits his style.

★ VIRGO (24th August – 23rd September) ★

Reliable and helpful, you like to think of other people's needs before your own. You are happy to let others take centre stage while you sit back and observe. You could be Liam's:

Best friend

You have the sweet qualities and kindness that appeal to Liam when it comes to having someone he can turn to. You'll always have his best interests at heart.

★ LIBRA (24th September – 23rd October) ★

Deep and romantic, you love being in love, and have an eye for the beautiful things in life. You could be Liam's:

Official photographer

Your eye for beauty is well suited to looking through the lens of a camera, as you photograph Liam in a variety of wonderful poses, exotic locations and different moods.

★ SCORPIO (24th October – 22nd November) ★

Wise and ambitious, you have a desire to succeed in life and are more than capable of getting to the top. You could be Liam's:

Career strategist

Your clever decision-making skills and step-by-step approach to success will always keep Liam at the top of his game and encourage him to explore new ventures.

★ SAGITTARIUS (23rd November – 21st December) ★

Full of life and enthusiasm, with a strong sense of adventure, you believe that the sky is the limit. All you have to do is to aim for it. You are happiest on the move. You could be Liam's:

Chauffeur
You love to be on the road, and driving Liam around, chatting with him as you do so, will give you great job satisfaction and happiness.

CAPRICORN (22nd December – 20th January)
Ambitious, with a good business brain, you have great patience and excellent organizational skills. You could be Liam's:

Social organizer
Be it party-planning or arranging his attendance at award ceremonies, charity events and celebrity weddings, you are the one charged with organizing the fun side of Liam's life.

AQUARIUS (21st January – 19th February)
Inventive and creative with an innovative streak, you also have a strong sense of right and wrong. You could be Liam's:

Personal shopper
Liam will enjoy your company and good judgement as you take him shopping for clothes. You love ethical fashion and will help him fight for what's right.

PISCES (20th February – 20th March)
Dreamy and creative, you are in touch with the mystical and sensual side of nature. You could be Liam's:

Astrologer
Your intuition and spiritual abilities, combined with vision and interpretation, will enable Liam to see what the future holds for him.

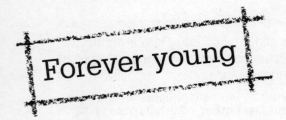

HOW MUCH DO YOU KNOW ABOUT LIAM'S LIFE BEFORE
HE WAS FAMOUS? CHECK YOUR ANSWERS ON **PAGE 92**.
TAKE THE TEST, IT'S CHILD'S PLAY!

1. Where is Liam from?
 a. Wolverhampton
 b. Birmingham
 c. Yorkshire

2. Who was Liam's karaoke favourite?
 a. The Beatles
 b. Robbie Williams
 c. Elvis Presley

3. What was his childhood pet dog called?
 a. Della
 b. Bella
 c. Stella

4. How did Liam mess around at school?
 a. He set off the fire alarm
 b. He hid his teacher's possessions
 c. He had water fights in the toilet

5. What did he say was his most embarrassing moment at school?

  a. Having his shorts and underpants pulled down during his school sports day

  b. His mum arriving at the school gates with a rain coat for him to wear

  c. Falling over on stage during a school play

6. Where did Liam do work experience?

  a. At a biscuit factory

  b. At an aircraft factory

  c. At a car factory

7. A keen sportsman, he narrowly missed out on a place in the England schools athletics team in which sport?

  a. Long jump

  b. Running

  c. High Jump

8. Name the performing arts group Liam joined.

  a. Pink Productions

  b. Peak Productions

  c. Play Productions

9. What show did he appear in with his performing arts group?

  a. *Saturday Night Fever*

  b. *Grease*

  c. *Guys and Dolls*

10. Which secondary school did he attend?

   a. St Barnaby's Senior

   b. St Paul's Comprehensive

   c. St Peter's Collegiate School

11. Which song did he sing with a friend in a school talent contest?

   a. 'Crazy' by Gnarls Barkley

   b. 'If I Could Turn Back The Hands Of Time' by R. Kelly

   c. 'Shine' by Take That

12. What sport did Liam take up to defend himself from bullies?

   a. Boxing

   b. Judo

   c. Kung Fu

13. He has two older sisters. What are their names?

   a. Georgia and Jess

   b. Zoe and Charlotte

   c. Nicola and Ruth

14. After school, what did Liam study at college?

   a. Drama

   b. Music

   c. Engineering

Sweet tweets

LIAM SHOWS HIS LOVE FOR HIS PARENTS AND HIS FANS
IN THIS SELECTION OF TWEETS. HE'S A BIG SOFTY AND
IS NOT AFRAID TO SHOW IT.

Happy Mothers Day to my lovely mum Karen :) She is the best.

Just cooking Chinese with my dad and he's got his new Gok Wan cook book yumm!!!

Guys I do really appreciate your support and love you all but sometimes it all gets too crazy for me.

Hey every1 who's tweetin I'll try and respond to every1 if u have a question or sumthin if I cant I'm sorry n I'm sure I'll get ya sum time soon xxx.

We have the best fans ever. Really appreciate your support. Will try and tweet back soon. x

Thank you to every one of you who helped get Little Things and Take Me Home to number 1! I love you all! You really are the best fans everrrr.

Thanks to everyone who's following. We shud have 1 huge group hug :D.

Cringe!

EVERYONE HAS EMBARRASSING MOMENTS IN LIFE THAT THEY'D RATHER FORGET. LOVELY LIAM IS HAPPY TO SHARE HIS WITH FANS. BUT CAN YOU TELL WHICH OF THESE STORIES ARE TRUE AND WHICH ARE FALSE? SEE HOW YOU DID ON **PAGE 92**.

1. Liam once forgot the lyrics to a song while performing on stage, so he tapped the microphone with his hand to pretend that it wasn't working.

☑ True Cringe ☐ Fake Fail

2. When asked by an interviewer if he would hang around the girls' changing rooms if he was invisible for the day, Liam replied, 'Do I look like the kind of girl who would do that? Did I just say girl? Oh no! It's been a long day. I do that all the time.'

☑ True Cringe ☐ Fake Fail

3. Liam used to have a pair of pink hair straighteners.

☑ True Cringe ☐ Fake Fail

4. Liam was so overwhelmed at meeting actor Will Smith that he couldn't speak and had to let his band mates do the talking instead.

☐ True Cringe   ☑ Fake Fail

5. He split his trousers on stage and had to perform to 9,000 people with a massive hole, showing off his Superman: Man of Steel boxer shorts.

☑ True Cringe   ☐ Fake Fail

6. He admits to still taking his beloved teddy bear with him on tour.

☐ True Cringe   ☑ Fake Fail

7. Liam once went to school wearing one black shoe and one brown. He didn't notice until he arrived and it was too late to go home and change.

☐ True Cringe   ☑ Fake Fail

FAIL!

Super-fans

ONE DIRECTION ALL AGREE THAT THEY HAVE THE BEST
FANS IN THE WORLD. SOME FAN ENCOUNTERS HAVE LEFT
THEM SHAKEN, BEWILDERED OR AMUSED. MARK WHICH
OF THESE STORIES ARE TRUE AND WHICH ARE FALSE.
CHECK YOUR ANSWERS ON **PAGE 92**.

1. One of the weirdest things that a fan has done to Liam
was to try to lick his face.

☑ True Tale ☐ Fan Fake

2. While Liam was surfing with Louis in Australia, a fan
gave him a toy shark.

☐ True Tale ☑ Fan Fake

3. He was startled to be shown a picture by a fan of her
dog, who she thought looked like him.

☐ True Tale ☑ Fan Fake

4. The boys were sent a box of carrots with their faces
drawn on them. As Liam is the tallest in the band, his
was the longest carrot, and Niall's was a carrot that
had been cut in half.

☑ True Tale ☐ Fan Fake

5. A fan ran past security into a building and shook Liam up by grabbing him.

☑ True Tale   ☐ Fan Fake

6. One of the most practical gifts he has been given by a fan is a Swiss Army Knife.

☐ True Tale   ☐ Fan Fake

7. A fan had to be led away by security after she kept insisting the band needed her as a lead singer. She wouldn't listen to them politely declining.

☐ True Tale   ☐ Fan Fake

8. Liam reckons Zayn is the quietest when the band is approached by fans, because he is really shy.

☐ True Tale   ☐ Fan Fake

9. A fan travelled to Liam's home town and spent the night in a sleeping bag outside what she thought was his parents' house. But it was the wrong house.

☐ True Tale   ☐ Fan Fake

10. The boys were being given a lift from Niagara Falls to a shopping arcade in a police car, when one misguided girl tried to break into the car and got arrested.

☐ True Tale   ☐ Fan Fake

11. Liam says that one of the nicest gifts he has been given by a fan was a figure of Woody from *Toy Story*.

☐ True Tale   ☐ Fan Fake

12. Liam was flattered when a fan told him that he was her favourite in One Direction. But he was left gobsmacked when she said, 'I love you, Louis.'

☐ True Tale ☐ Fan Fake

13. He once signed an autograph as 'Justin Bieber' after a girl refused to believe that he wasn't Bieber.

☐ True Tale ☐ Fan Fake

14. Liam was confused when a fan told him that she didn't really like One Direction very much but could she have his autograph anyway.

☐ True Tale ☐ Fan Fake

Twitterverse

LIAM JUST CAN'T STOP BEING A BIG TWIT,
AND HE'S NOT AFRAID WHO KNOWS IT!
HERE ARE SOME OF HIS FUNNIEST TWEETS.

Nananananana batmannnn.

Wish I had the confidence to talk to people.

I have growing pains lol.

Postman Pat, Postman Pat, Postman Pat and his black and white cattt ...

Sat next to the Niallanator in the car ... Gosh those legs are ferocious!

I am the flashing toothbrush master.

You only love me for my flashing toothbrush ha.

Not to alarm anyone but I genuinely think I have left my toothbrush in the last place we were in.

So to start the day off I've spilt Lucozade all over my jeans I'm too clumsy.

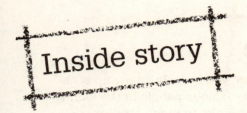

Inside story

THE TOP SHOWBIZ JOURNALISTS IN THE COUNTRY ARE
INVITED TO A TOP HOTEL IN LONDON TO INTERVIEW
LIAM PAYNE AT A PRESS CONFERENCE.

The pressure's on – the editor of your college magazine
wants an exclusive. What do you ask Liam? Fill in the
blanks in the story below.

Entering the hotel you are ushered into the grand reception
room and join the journalists gathered on rows of chairs.
A few minutes later, Liam walks in with a PR, smiles, says
'Hello, thanks for coming,' and sits at the top table. The
journalists are invited to ask Liam questions. Determined
to make your mark, you raise a hand and the publicist tells
you to go ahead. You say:

'Hi Liam. I'm .... from ....'

Liam smiles and says: '... .'

Your first question makes him laugh. You ask: '...................
.... ?'

Liam replies '...
.... ,'

While you have his attention, you quickly follow up with
another question. 'Which six famous people in the world
– still living – would you most like to invite for dinner?'

Liam thinks about this for a while and then answers:
'...
....
.... ,'

The publicist looks around the room, keen to get other
journalists involved, but you manage to squeeze in one
more question. It's a really good one. You cheekily ask:
'.. ?'

Liam smiles and answers: '...
.... ,'

As other journalists ask their questions, you listen to
Liam's replies and raise your hand a few times. But it looks
like you may not get another chance. Before you know
it, the press conference has ended. You have some great
stories, but your editor is hard to please. It's no use you
giving her the same story all the other journalists got. She
wants an exclusive. And that means, somehow, you have to
get Liam on his own. But how?

Liam thanks everyone and gets up from the table. He leaves the room as the journalists file out through another door. All apart from you. Quietly, you circle the room and then slip out of the same door that Liam used.

At first you can't see him, but then you turn a corner and spot him up ahead with the publicist. Suddenly, they stop and turn. You hear Liam say, 'My hat. I left it on the table.' The PR says she will get it for him. You quickly open a door and find yourself in a large storage room full of boxes, stacked chairs and brooms. You jump when you hear a knock on the door. Oh, no! The PR has seen you. Now, you're in trouble. You open the door sheepishly and there, to your astonishment, stands Liam.

'I thought I saw you,' he smiles, stepping into the room. 'Was there anything you wanted?'

You reply that your editor wants you to get an exclusive and you were hoping to ask him a few extra questions. Liam closes the door and says, 'Go ahead. Ask away.'

You can't believe your luck and want to ask a question that might be a headline-grabbing feature – if he gives a good answer. So, taking a deep breath, you ask: '.............................
.... ?'

Liam looks a little taken aback but then answers carefully:
'..
....

.... ,

You're delighted. This is wonderful. You follow up with:

'..

.... ?'

And Liam replies: '...

....

....'

Well, it doesn't get better than that. Even the editor will love this exclusive.

You hear a shuffling outside and Liam says it's probably the publicist waiting for him. 'I'll go out first,' he says, 'and tell her I got lost. Then, when the coast is clear, you can slip away. I promise I won't tell.'

'Thank you so much,' you reply.

'I hope you got a good story,' he says.

You smile and reply, 'And I hope you get your hat back!'

Now turn the page and write up your dream interview with Liam.

EXCLUSIVE INTERVIEW WITH LIAM

by _____ (write your name)

_____

_____

_____

_____

_____

_____

_____

_____

_____

_____

_____

_____

_____

_____

_____

_____

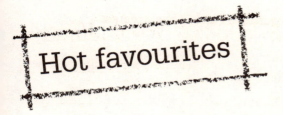

Hot favourites

LIAM MAY BE YOUR FAVOURITE THING IN LIFE, BUT DO YOU KNOW HIS FAVOURITE THINGS? TRY THIS QUIZ TO SEE IF YOU KNOW WHAT MAKES HIM HAPPY. CHECK YOUR ANSWERS ON **PAGE 93**.

1. Which is Liam's favourite boy band?
- **a.** JLS
- **b.** The Wanted
- **c.** *NSYNC

2. Which of these films does he love the most?
- **a.** *Monsters, Inc.*
- **b.** The *Toy Story* trilogy
- **c.** *The Incredibles*

3. If he could swap places with another celebrity, who would it be?
- **a.** Johnny Depp
- **b.** Will Smith
- **c.** Simon Cowell

4. Who did Liam describe as one of the greatest entertainers ever?

   a. Michael Jackson

   b. Robbie Williams

   c. Paul McCartney

5. Which of these is his favourite TV reality star?

   a. Kim Kardashian in *Keeping Up With The Kardashians*

   b. Ozzy Osbourne in *The Osbournes*

   c. Stephanie Pratt in *The Hills*

6. What is his favourite food when in the USA?

   a. Cheeseburger

   b. Key lime pie

   c. Hot dog

7. Which superhero would he most like to be?

   a. Spider-man

   b. Superman

   c. Iron Man

8. Which is his favourite song on the band's *Up All Night* album?

   a. 'One Thing'

   b. 'Gotta Be You'

   c. 'More Than This'

9. Which of these is one his favourite treats?
- **a.** Double chocolate brownie
- **b.** Doughnut
- **c.** Chocolate peanut-butter torte

10. What did he say was his favourite chat-up line?
- **a.** 'How are you doing?'
- **b.** 'Hi, I'm Liam. What's yours?'
- **c.** 'Fancy going somewhere else?'

11. When it comes to hair colour, which girl does Liam prefer?
- **a.** Brunette
- **b.** Redhead
- **c.** Blonde

12. Which movie franchise would he most like an acting role in?
- **a.** James Bond
- **b.** X-Men
- **c.** Pirates of the Caribbean

13. What is Liam's favourite Beatles' song?
- **a.** 'Help!'
- **b.** 'Love Me Do'
- **c.** 'Penny Lane'

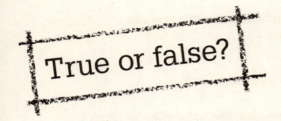

ALL THE FACTS BELOW ARE TRUE, BUT NOT ALL
OF THEM ARE ABOUT LIAM. CAN YOU TELL WHICH
ONES ARE? FOR EXTRA POINTS, FILL IN THE NAME
OF THE BAND MEMBER THE FALSE FACTS APPLY TO.
THE ANSWERS ARE ON **PAGE 93**.

1. Liam fancies himself as a bit of a cook and is
particularly proud of his Chinese curry. He makes the
sauce from scratch using his dad's recipe.

☐ True ☐ False. It is ....

2. Liam got stung on the foot by a sea urchin while at a
judge's house on *The X Factor*.

☐ True ☐ False. It was ....

3. Liam has two pet miniature turtles.

☐ True ☐ False. It is ....

4. Liam once had a dream that he was playing football in
a Champions League final with David Beckham.

☐ True ☐ False. It was ....

5. Liam found the book *To Kill A Mockingbird* by Harper Lee a little confusing because, 200 pages in, the bird still isn't dead.

☐ True   ☐ False. It was ....

6. Liam used to enjoy reading his horoscope when he was younger and now wants to get his palm read.

☐ True   ☐ False. It is ....

7. Liam says he annoys himself because he uses the words 'brilliant' and 'fantastic' too often.

☐ True   ☐ False. It is ....

8. Liam hates wasps, particularly after being stung by one in a painful place!

☐ True   ☐ False. It is ....

9. Liam hates asparagus.

☐ True   ☐ False. It is ....

10. Liam's *X Factor* audition number was #165616.

☐ True   ☐ False. It was ....

Your theme song

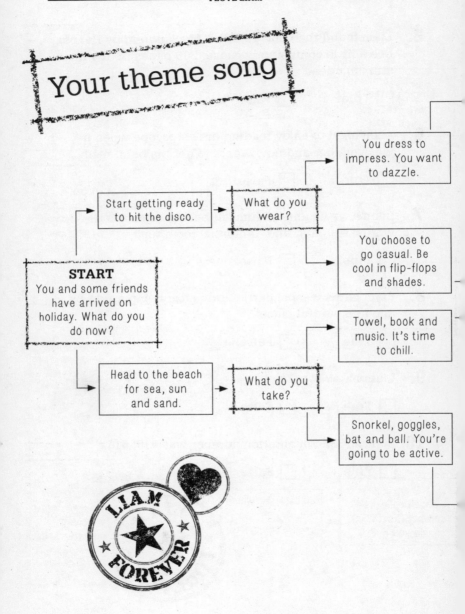

START
You and some friends have arrived on holiday. What do you do now?

Start getting ready to hit the disco.

What do you wear?

You dress to impress. You want to dazzle.

You choose to go casual. Be cool in flip-flops and shades.

Head to the beach for sea, sun and sand.

What do you take?

Towel, book and music. It's time to chill.

Snorkel, goggles, bat and ball. You're going to be active.

LIAM FOREVER

You spot someone dancing on their own. What do you do?

→ Go over and ask if they fancy dancing with you and your friends.

→ **'Back For You'**
Confident and outgoing, you are fun to be around. You are certainly not the shy type. You know what you want and you go for it.

→ Smile and hope that they come over and join you.

→ **'Gotta Be You'**
You remain upbeat despite set backs and are determined to dust yourself off and carry on again. That's what your friends like most about you.

→ Hurry home and dry off before going out again.

It starts raining and you get drenched. What do you do?

→ Laugh and carry on having fun.

→ **'Summer Love'**
Live for the moment and have as much fun as possible — that's your motto. Long-term plans can wait until later. You relish what life throws at you.

→ Join in, the more the merrier.

There's a beach volleyball competition. What do you do?

→ Sit back and watch others playing, while sipping a cool drink.

→ **'I Would'**
You sure know how to chill out! Relaxed and easy-going, you do your own thing, seldom lose your temper and don't get too worried about the stresses in life.

What was the question?

LIAM HAS BEEN ASKED ALL SORTS OF WEIRD AND WONDERFUL QUESTIONS IN INTERVIEWS. HERE ARE SOME OF HIS REPLIES. CAN YOU MATCH EACH OF THEM TO THE CORRECT QUESTION? WATCH OUT, THERE ARE SOME FAKE QUESTIONS.
TURN TO **PAGE 93** TO SEE HOW YOU DID.

Liam's Answers:

1. 'I'd just hop on a plane and fly to anywhere in the world. No one would know. You could go on holiday.'

2. 'Zayn loves to leave the car window open in the morning when it's absolutely freezing in the UK and I'm sat there – like my seat, we have our own designated seats in the car ...'

3. 'Most of the time that's how I find things out! With Harry, everything happens so quickly. Harry is actually quite secretive. He tells us some things, but others he keeps secret.'

4. 'Can we get waxworks at Madame Tussauds? We've never thought about that.'

5. 'Parallel parking for the first time.'

Questions:

A. You already have your own action figures – what other merchandise do you aspire to?

B. What's it like reading about the other guys' love lives in the papers?

C. If you could be anonymous for the day, what would you do right now?

D. What's your proudest moment so far?

E. Is there any competitiveness between you all about doing wild things?

F. If you were invisible for the day, what would you do?

G. What do you like and dislike about each other?

H. Of all the things you have done in life, what has made your mum the most proud?

Write your answers here:

1. ....   **3.** ....   **5.** ....

2. ....   **4.** ....

Stole my heart

EVERYONE KNOWS LIAM IS CUTE, SENSITIVE, CARING AND AS SOFT AS A PUPPY.

HAVE A LOOK AT THESE STORIES AND RATE THEM ON THE 'CUTE-O-METER' BELOW.

Cute-O-Meter

♥♡♡♡♡ Aww

♥♥♡♡♡ What A Cutie!

♥♥♥♡♡ Super Sweet

♥♥♥♥♡ Cuteness Overload

♥♥♥♥♥ I Can't Even Cope With How Cute That Is!

Girls go crazy for Liam, but he is still nervous about meeting celebrities:

'I'd say I was quite shy, although it doesn't look it when there's cameras and stuff. But if I ask a star for a photo with them, I'm not very good at all. I just haven't got the confidence.'

Liam is extremely generous, especially when it comes to his family:

'I'm not an extravagant person, but I got my dad a car.'

Liam was moved when he and his One Direction band mates met some seriously ill children and spent the day playing and having fun with them:

'It's such a small thing for us, but the kids get so much out of it. We really love doing things like this. We leave smiling because they are always so wonderful.'

He is a big animal lover and particularly likes dogs. So a soppy movie about a dog had him blubbing:

The one movie that made me cry — it's got to be Marley & Me — it's just a sad movie about a really nice dog.

He may be one of the most successful singers around, but Liam was still worried about what his parents would think about him getting a tattoo:

I'm making plans to get one — but don't tell my parents.

When asked what is the one thing that always puts a smile on his face, Liam replied:

Louis. Whatever happens he'll just make me laugh about something because he's just that crazy.

What's the best thing about being in One Direction? International stardom? Wealth? Nah. It's simpler than that:

'Probably that we've all made four new best mates.'

For his eighteenth birthday, Liam asked his fans to think of others and not him. He tweeted:

'For my birthday I would like everyone to visit cancerresearchuk.org and donate as much as they can to help fight cancer.'

He's a lad who likes giving rather than receiving. That's what pleases him:

'When it comes to birthdays I don't care how much it costs if it makes you happy.'

What a day!

IF YOU COULD GET PAID FOR DAYDREAMING ABOUT
HANGING OUT WITH LIAM, YOU'D BE A MILLIONAIRE.
IT'S TIME TO DESCRIBE YOUR PERFECT DAY WITH HIM.
WHERE WOULD YOU GO? WHAT WOULD YOU WEAR?
WOULD YOU INTRODUCE HIM TO YOUR FRIENDS OR KEEP
HIM ALL TO YOURSELF? WRITE IT DOWN HERE.

Need some help getting started?

Try to include the answers to these questions:

- How would your day start?
- What do you love most about Liam?
- Where would you take him?
- What would he wear?
- What would you eat together?
- What would you say to him?
- What would you want to ask him?
- What would you want him to ask you?
- How would your day end?

A delicious date

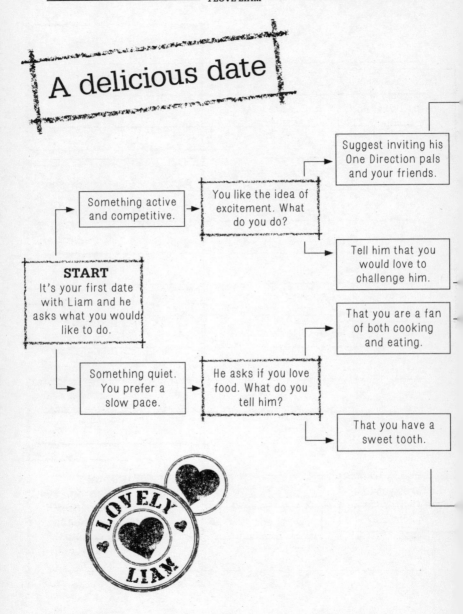

START
It's your first date with Liam and he asks what you would like to do.

Something active and competitive.

You like the idea of excitement. What do you do?

Suggest inviting his One Direction pals and your friends.

Tell him that you would love to challenge him.

Something quiet. You prefer a slow pace.

He asks if you love food. What do you tell him?

That you are a fan of both cooking and eating.

That you have a sweet tooth.

LOVELY LIAM

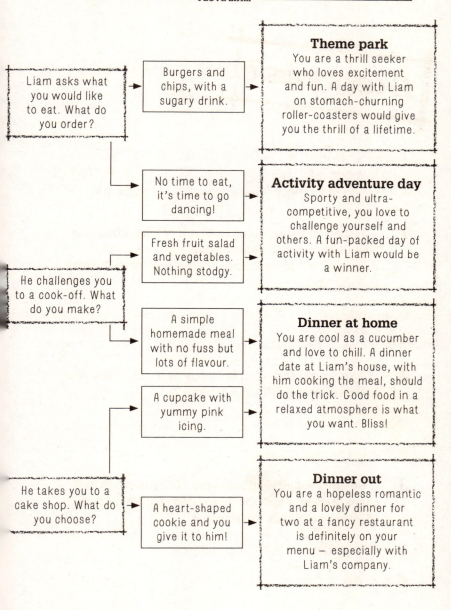

Liam asks what you would like to eat. What do you order?

Burgers and chips, with a sugary drink.

Theme park
You are a thrill seeker who loves excitement and fun. A day with Liam on stomach-churning roller-coasters would give you the thrill of a lifetime.

No time to eat, it's time to go dancing!

Activity adventure day
Sporty and ultra-competitive, you love to challenge yourself and others. A fun-packed day of activity with Liam would be a winner.

He challenges you to a cook-off. What do you make?

Fresh fruit salad and vegetables. Nothing stodgy.

A simple homemade meal with no fuss but lots of flavour.

Dinner at home
You are cool as a cucumber and love to chill. A dinner date at Liam's house, with him cooking the meal, should do the trick. Good food in a relaxed atmosphere is what you want. Bliss!

A cupcake with yummy pink icing.

He takes you to a cake shop. What do you choose?

A heart-shaped cookie and you give it to him!

Dinner out
You are a hopeless romantic and a lovely dinner for two at a fancy restaurant is definitely on your menu – especially with Liam's company.

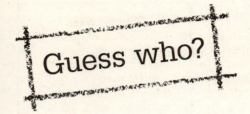

Guess who?

READ THE QUOTES FROM LIAM BELOW AND SEE IF YOU CAN WORK OUT WHO OR WHAT HE IS TALKING ABOUT. YOU'LL FIND THE ANSWERS ON **PAGE 93**.

1. 'I've had to bang on his door a few times because he's playing loud music at like 1 o'clock in the morning.' Which member of One Direction is Liam talking about?

Clue: This guy is quiff-tastic as well as noisy.

Who was he talking about? ....

2. 'Taylor is neutral. Can be a boy or a girl.' Why was Liam so interested in this name?

Clue: What a broody boy!

What was he talking about? ....

3. 'They get some good presents. They don't expect them. I know I bought them iPads for Christmas.' Who was lucky at Christmas?

Clue: Oh brother, he's a generous boy!

Who is it? ....

4. 'My biggest news today. I met one of my idols and couldn't even look him in the eye,' Liam tweeted and posted a picture of him with which US singer?

Clue: This guy is a rapper with a famous wife.

Who was he talking about? ....

5. 'I don't know … He thinks differently. He's on a different wavelength to everybody else I find, sometimes … and I'd love to discover why.' This was Liam's reply when asked who he would like to swap lives with in the band for a day. But who was it?

Clue: Is he different because he was born in a different country to the other lads?

Who is it? ....

6. 'He never gets out of bed. In fact, he was third into the car today, so he did quite well, but he is incredibly lazy. He's not lazy in an "I can't be bothered to get you a drink" way, just in the way he sleeps, because he's always the last to get up.' Who did Liam mean?

Clue: He probably takes longest to get ready, too.

Who was he talking about? ....

7. '[It's] all about like being spontaneous, carefree, just, you know, like living life and having fun sort of thing, I suppose, like living for the moment. Kind of Louis's motto.' What song was Liam referring to?

Clue: A great start to the album.

Which track was he talking about? ....

Last first kiss

DESPITE HIS FAME AND BEING ADORED BY LEGIONS OF FANS, LIAM ADMITS TO BEING TONGUE-TIED WHEN IT COMES TO GIRLS. HERE'S WHAT HE THINKS OF LOVE, ROMANCE AND ALL THINGS SOPPY.

When it comes to Valentine's Day, he likes to make an extra special effort:

'One Valentine's Day, my girlfriend at the time insisted all she wanted was one of my hoodies. I thought, "That's a bit rubbish," so I bought a box, put the hoodie inside with a teddy bear, 12 red roses and a Justin Bieber CD.'

He enjoys cooking for a girl, but doesn't like to make a meal of it:

'If I was cooking for a girl, I'd make fajitas because they're simple and your date can pick what she wants, so there's no pressure.'

He denied he was dating his fellow *X-Factor* contestant Leona Lewis, but is not too shy to admit that he fancies her. When asked which celebrity he fancied, he replied:

'Leona Lewis. She's hot and seems like a nice person.'

Sometimes beauty really is skin deep when it comes to attractiveness. A big turn-off for Liam when it comes to girls is:

> '*Too much fake tan. Orange hands, no one likes orange hands.*'

Liam's two older sisters 'married him off' at a young age when he first kissed a girl who lived next door:

> '*My sister decided it would be a good idea to play "getting married". My parents turned up and everything.*'

Being a shy lad he likes to keep things fun and easy-going on a first date, and his ideal place to take a girl is:

> '*Bowling or the cinema. The cinema saves all that awkward conversation.*'

He believes in trying again if a girl turns him down but realizes that there is a point where you have to give up:

> '*I think you have to keep trying for a bit because you don't know if they're just playing games with you. They might be testing to see if you really care about them. If they stop answering your calls though, it's time to move on!*'

His first proper kiss was jaw-dropping:

> '*I don't remember much, so it can't have been great! I was 11 or 12 and I remember knocking teeth, but I think I got the hang of it!*'

Liam admits he finds it easier to flirt over the phone:

'I'm not good at speaking to girls. I'd much rather get their number and text them.'

The girl to win his heart doesn't have to look like this, but it might give them an advantage:

'My perfect girl would probably have curly hair, errm, she would have blue eyes maybe. Light browny, kinda blondy hair.'

Practice makes perfect – even if there's no one around to practise on:

'I used to practise snogging on the back of my hand. I'm not embarrassed. Everyone's done it!'

Spot the difference

Can you find eight differences between the top and bottom pictures?
You can check your answers on page 94.

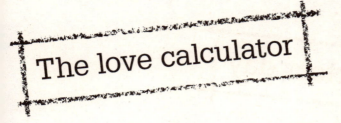

The love calculator

HERE IS A FAST AND FUN WAY TO WORK OUT WHETHER YOU ARE LIAM'S PERFECT MATCH.

Write your name and his with 'LOVES' in the middle. Then write down in a row how many letter 'L's, 'O's, 'V's, 'E's and 'S's there are in both your names (ignore the word 'loves'). Add together pairs of numbers – the first and the second, the second and the third, and so on – to work out a final 'percentage'. This tells you how likely you are to be Liam's dream girl.

Here's an example:

JAN LAVERNE  LIAM PAYNE

There are two 'L's, zero 'O's, one 'V', three 'E's and zero 'S's.

Write this as: 2 0 1 3 0

Add together each pair of numbers until you have only two left.

$$
\begin{array}{c}
2\ 0\ 1\ 3\ 0 \\
2\ 1\ 4\ 3 \\
3\ 5\ 7 \\
8\ 1\ 2 \\
93\%
\end{array}
$$

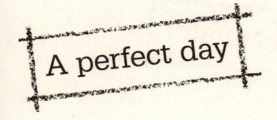

A perfect day

YOU MAY HAVE DREAMED ABOUT HELPING OUT YOUR FAVOURITE MEMBER OF ONE DIRECTION IN HIS HOUR OF NEED, AND THIS ADVENTURE STORY PUTS YOU IN THE DRIVING SEAT.

It's Monday morning, and you forgot to set the alarm.

Mum calls up the stairs and you drag yourself out of bed, throw on some clothes, and grab a slice of toast as you rush out of the door with a quick, 'Bye Mum. Bye Dad.'

Outside the house, you see your shiny new scooter, a gift from your parents for passing the motorbike driving test. But college is very close, and your pride and joy will be safer at home, so you decide to walk.

Strolling round the corner, still daydreaming about the great weekend you've just had with your pals, you're surprised to see a flashy black car, with dark smoky windows, parked by the kerb.

A man in a smart suit is tinkering under the bonnet and muttering under his breath. As you approach, the back window opens and a familiar-looking face appears.

'Any luck, Jeff?' asks the guy inside. You stop in your tracks.

It can't be! It is!

It's Liam Payne.

'Sorry, Liam,' yells the driver. 'It's not looking good. I need to take it to a garage straight away, but I'll have to call someone to tow it.'

'But I need to be in the next town for the gig tonight!' Liam despairs. 'What are we going to do?'

Just then the driver spots you. 'Do you live around here?' he asks. 'Can you help us? Do you know where the nearest garage is?'

As it happens, your dad, who was tucking into his breakfast when you left the house, is a great car mechanic.

After hastily rearranging your hair and straightening your clothes, what do you do?

Decide between the following options:

1. You offer to fetch your dad to fix the car on the spot. Go to **A** below.

2. You ask Liam if he wants a lift on the back of your scooter. Go to **B** on **page 59**.

A: Liam winds the window down further. 'That's really kind of you,' he says, flashing a killer smile. 'Do you think he'd mind? We'll make sure he is paid well.'

'Of c-c-c-course he won't mind,' you stammer, nervously, wishing you had worn your favourite jeans this morning and realizing this may be your chance to put matters right. 'I won't be a minute.'

As calmly as possible, you stroll round the corner. But as soon as you are sure you're out of sight, you break into a run, eager to get back home.

Bursting through the door, you blurt out the whole story to your dad, who laughs as he grabs his tool kit and says, 'I'll see what I can do. You coming?'

You reply, 'Right behind you.'

As he leaves, you pop upstairs to brush your hair and change your trousers. Before you can say 'That's What Makes You Beautiful', you're out of the door and heading round the corner.

Finding your dad bent over the engine, sucking his teeth and shaking his head, you can tell it's going to take a while.

'It's a bit of a job,' your dad says. 'I can fix it, but it'll take a couple of hours.'

'That's okay,' says Liam. 'As long as I'm there by this afternoon, it's cool.'

Then he turns to you and asks, 'So what is there to do around here? Looks like I've got a little time to kill.'

What do you suggest?

Decide between the following options:

1. You suggest a walk in the park followed by a civilized lunch. Go to **A1** below.

2. You feel like having fun – and ice skating sounds like a great idea. Go to **A2** on **page 56**.

A1: 'Good idea,' beams Liam. 'I could do with some fresh air. A walk sounds perfect.' Suddenly his face falls. 'There won't be too many people about, will there?'

'I doubt it,' you reassure him. 'The local park is pretty empty in the daytime. Just a couple of dog-walkers.'

Liam agrees and pulls on his coat and a beanie hat. 'Come on then,' he says. 'Show me the sights.'

At the park gates, Liam stops while you check the coast is clear, then strolls across the grass with you chatting and asking about your college course. Suddenly, he sees a pile of autumn leaves and breaks into a run. 'Come on,' he yells, grabbing handfuls of the brown and yellow leaves and throwing them over you as you approach.

'Hey!' you laugh, chucking some back at him. A full leaf-fight breaks out, and the pair of you are so giggly you fail to notice a group of girls coming towards you.

As soon you spot them, you stop with an inner groan. It's some friends from college, on their way through the park to look for you after you didn't turn up this morning.

What do you do?

Decide between the following options:

1. You duck through the woods to avoid your friends and keep Liam to yourself. Go to **A1a** below.

2. You casually introduce him to your pals because you can't resist showing off. Go to **A1b** on **page 55**.

A1a: 'I know those girls. They're bound to let the secret out if they know you're here,' you tell Liam. 'Perhaps we'd better get out of here before they see you.'

'Which way?' he asks.

'Follow me,' you answer, and the pair of you run, breathless and laughing, through the woods.

When you emerge at a side gate, the others are nowhere to be seen, and Liam stops to get his breath back.

'How about lunch then?' he grins.

'Great. There's a quiet little café round the corner.'

Over lunch you chat some more and, as Liam tucks into a bacon sandwich, your phone rings. It's your dad telling you the car's fixed.

As you tell Liam the news, you look a little sad that your adventure is over, until he sees the look on your face.

'You've been brilliant,' he pipes up. 'How about you and your friends come to the show tonight and meet the lads?'

Fantastic. A chance to see him again AND make it up to your pals!

THE END

A1b: 'They're friends of mine, actually,' you tell Liam. 'They must be looking for me. I could get rid of them if you like.'

'Not at all,' insists Liam. 'Any friend of yours is a friend of mine. Let's say hi.'

You stroll over to the three girls as casually as your wobbly legs will allow, and introduce the 1D star.

'Hi, this is Liam.'

One of your friends stretches out a hand, 'It's nice to meet ...' Her voice trails off as she realizes her companions are standing in open-mouthed awe and the penny drops.

The singer shakes her hand and smiles, 'Nice to meet you all. We were just off to grab a bite to eat. Wanna join us?'

The flustered threesome turn pink as they accept the invitation and look amazed as Liam turns to you and asks, 'Where to, boss?'

You suggest a quiet little bistro run by a friend of your dad's, where you know Liam won't be bothered, and off you go.

As you eat, your dad calls to say the car is fixed and Liam can move on.

'Thanks so much,' he says. 'I've had great fun here today. Maybe you girls could come with me – I'll introduce you to the rest of the band.'

None of you needs to be asked twice ... what a perfect day!

THE END

A2: 'Sounds like fun,' says Liam. 'I haven't skated for years. Let's do it.'

'I'm a pretty good skater,' you boast. 'I'll show you how.'

Leaving Dad to fiddle with the motor, you stroll happily to the ice rink, which happens to be just a few streets away. It's always pretty quiet in the afternoon, so you hope you can have Liam all to yourself.

At the rink, you smoothly strap on your blades, as he struggles to do the straps on his.

'Here, let me help,' you offer, bursting with confidence.

'Thanks,' he smiles shyly. 'I hope I can stay upright.'

'It's easy once you get the swing of it,' you reassure him, secretly hoping he'll need to hold your hand to get round.

He timidly tiptoes on to the ice as you glide elegantly out. Then he wobbles, and you hold out a hand, which he gratefully takes – sending a blush through your cold cheeks.

'Okay,' you mutter. 'See if you can straighten up. We'll take it slow ...'

After a couple of practices, he seems to be grasping it when, horror of horrors ... you completely stack it, landing on the floor, in a crumpled, wet, heap. You see Liam trying not to laugh. What do you do?

Decide between the following options:

1. You hold back the tears, suggest that it's time to go and get out as quickly as possible. Go to **A2a** below.

2. You laugh at your own misfortune ... you shouldn't have bragged after all. Go to **A2b** on **page 58**.

A2a: Liam's face turns from laughter to concern as he looks down at you on the ice.

'Sorry,' he says. 'Are you alright? Are you hurt?'

'Only my pride,' you mutter miserably. 'I don't usually fall over.'

He offers a hand to pull you up. As you take it, he tumbles over too and the pair of you sit on the ice, laughing like kids.

'Come on,' he says. 'I fancy a hot chocolate. I'm no good at this.'

At the rink side, he buys the hot drinks and you sit and chat, amazed at how much you have in common.

All too soon, your mobile rings and your dad tells you the car is ready to roll.

Heading back, you are lost in the unhappy certainty you will soon have to say goodbye to Liam, when he breaks into your thoughts.

'You've really helped me out today,' he says. 'And I've had a great time. How do you fancy coming to the gig tonight as our VIP guest?'

A great day just got even better.

THE END

A2b: Despite your wet bottom and dented ego, you dissolve into giggles on the ice and Liam looks relieved.

'Are you okay? I felt awful laughing but I couldn't help it.'

'Course not,' you smile. 'My own fault for bigging myself up so much. I'm actually quite an average skater.'

'You're still better than me,' he insists, taking your hand again to help you up from the ice. 'Let's start again.'

After a few more laps of the rink, his technique is improving and you've managed to impress with a few fancy moves, making up for the earlier embarrassment.

It's getting late, and Liam begins to look worried, so you call time on the skating session and head back to the car.

When you get there, your dad is sharing a cup of tea with the driver. The car is all fixed.

'I can't thank you enough,' the 1D star says to your dad. Then, turning to you, he adds, 'Or you. I have had the most brilliant afternoon. If you're free tonight, why don't you and your family come along for the show and for a party backstage afterwards?'

Your perfect day just got even better.

THE END

B: The door of the car opens and Liam steps out. He's looking as gorgeous as ever in jeans and a T-shirt with a denim shirt thrown over the top.

'That sounds like fun,' he grins. 'I'll try anything once.'

'G-g-great,' you stammer, thinking that at least your helmet will hide the bad-hair-day mess you've got going on. 'I'll just pop home and fetch my scooter and some helmets.'

'I'll walk with you,' Liam says, and you stroll down the road in a daze, hardly daring to believe your favourite 1D star is walking beside you.

At your house, you quickly fly upstairs to pick up the helmets and take the opportunity to straighten your hair. Back outside, you realize your spare helmet is purple with orange flowers.

'My favourite colours,' grins Liam. 'Good job I don't have hair like Harry's though.'

Liam tells you the name of the venue. You climb on to the scooter and he puts his arms round your waist. You breathe a sigh of relief that he can't see the silly grin on your face as you start up the engine – and you're off.

As you zoom along the lanes, you imagine the wind flying through your hair as Liam clings on with an adoring look on his face.

But you're so busy daydreaming, you miss a turning and before you know it, you're miles out of the way and totally lost.

What will you do now?

Decide between the following options:

1. You confess that you're lost and phone for help. Go to **B1** below.

2. You risk it and carry on, hoping you see a signpost soon. Go to **B2** on **page 63**.

B1: You stop in the nearest lay-by and cut the engine. Liam takes off his helmet and asks, 'What's wrong?'

Nervous, you go for a corny joke: 'Well, you know we were going in One Direction? We should have been going in the other direction!'

Liam frowns, and you instantly regret making light of the situation – until he cracks a smile.

'Good joke, but can you find the right direction?' he asks.

'I'll call home. My dad will know the way,' you reassure him, reaching for your mobile.

A quick chat and you're back on the right road. You soon find the right street but, as you approach the venue, Liam's grip tightens. A crowd of screaming fans are outside and he doesn't want to be mobbed. What do you do?

Decide between the following options:

1. You turn up a side street and take him away from the arena to plan your next move. Go to **B1a** below.

2. You brave the crowd and go to the security gate, hoping they won't notice Liam with his helmet on. Go to **B1b** on **page 62**.

B1a: Before the crowd gets a chance to spot your VIP passenger, you take a left down a residential street.

At the end of the road, you see a turning for a secluded car park and stop to hatch a plan.

'Phew, that was close,' says Liam. 'I would never have got through the crowd if they'd spotted me.'

'Okay, so what next?' you ask. 'Any ideas?'

'Give me a moment,' Liam says, and pulls out his phone. He dials and then chats away to someone on the other end. 'Round the corner ... Leafy Lane ... a friend brought me ... a scooter.'

He soon hangs up and says, 'Security are sending a van. Won't be long.'

'A van? Why not a car?' you ask.

'Well, how would we fit your scooter in the car?' he laughs. 'You didn't think I was ready to say goodbye just yet, did you? You have to come and meet the lads, and see the gig.'

As the van swings round the corner, it's not the scooter racing any more – it's your heart.

THE END

B1b: 'Hang on and keep you head down,' you yell at Liam. 'I'll get you through this crowd.'

A muffled 'thanks' comes from behind you.

Seeing a gate marked 'Security', you head that way and slow down as you reach the back of the crowd. 'Coming through!' you shout, in your bossiest voice. 'Clear the way.'

The fans begin to part to make way for you, and Liam ducks his head so he can't be seen. Arriving at the gate, you are stopped by a burly guard, who grunts, 'Passes.'

As quietly as you can you tell him, 'I've got one of the band on the back – Liam.'

'How gullible do you think I am?' laughs the guard.

'It's true. It's me,' confirms the singer as he whips off the helmet. 'Quick, let us in.'

A shout of 'LIAM!' goes up behind him, and the crowd

surges forward. It's all the confirmation the guard needs, and quick as a flash, he opens the gate as you sail through.

You park the scooter outside the stage door, and Liam beckons you to follow as it swings open. Inside, you are greeted by four familiar faces – Harry, Zayn, Louis and Niall.

After introducing you, Liam says, 'You saved me – twice in one day. You had better stay and watch the show now. I'm expecting to see you when I get off stage.'

Your heart is bursting with excitement – it doesn't get better than this.

THE END

B2: Your heart is pumping as you realize you are lost but you were never one to admit your mistakes, and there's no way you are going to make a U-turn. Maybe if you plough on he won't notice you have gone the wrong way.

After 15 minutes, you are beginning to panic. You are getting further away from the venue and have no way of turning off the road.

Then you spot a sign. There's a turning in the right direction up ahead. Phew! Hoping he'll be none the wiser, you motor on towards the venue.

Hitting the outskirts of town, you get your bearings. You know your way to the arena but you're already hating the thought of saying goodbye to your precious passenger.

You arrive all too soon. As Liam climbs off the scooter, he turns to you and says, 'I can't thank you enough. You saved my skin. I'm quite early, so do you want to hang out with the lads? Or shall we sneak off for a quiet meal?'

Wow! The hardest choice of your life. So which will it be?

Decide between the following options:

1. You want to keep Liam to yourself for a couple more hours. Go to **B2a** below.

2. You want to hang out with the lads. Go to **B2b** on **page 65**.

B2a: 'I was hoping you'd say that,' says Liam. 'It'll be nice to have a proper chat after being on the back of the bike all that time.'

Sitting down in an exclusive restaurant around the corner from the venue, you find you both have plenty to talk about.

As you tuck into the main meal, Liam leans in and asks, 'Can I ask you something? Did you get lost on the way here?'

You flush with embarrassment, then giggle. 'A little. I was hoping you wouldn't notice.'

He laughs and you relax again, and minutes later you're engrossed in conversation when he suddenly jumps up. 'Oh, I've got to go. I need to go for the sound-check before the gig.'

You stand up, too, and he leaves plenty of cash to cover the bill before you both hurry out. As you reach the venue, he hugs you and says, 'Thanks for being a lifesaver. You are going to come to the gig, aren't you?'

Well, you could hardly say no.

THE END

B2b: 'I'm not that hungry,' you answer. 'Would you mind if we met up with the band?'

'Course not,' replies Liam. 'Come on in.'

Inside the arena, you can't believe your eyes. The massive stage is set for the show, and people are rushing about seeing to last-minute details.

Backstage, he leads you through a door marked 'VIPs only'.

'About time, too,' shouts a voice – which turns out to be Harry Styles.

'Where have you been, Liam?' chimes in Niall, then seeing you adds, 'Oh, I see.'

Liam laughs and tells them the whole story, and the four lads crowd round you, thanking you for bringing Liam over. Then he suddenly gives you a hug.

'You are my guardian angel,' he says. 'Make sure you stay and watch us all tonight.'

A perfect end to a perfect day.

THE END

Would you rather?

JUST HANGING OUT WITH LIAM IS MORE THAN ENOUGH
FUN FOR MOST PEOPLE, BUT IF YOU COULD CHOOSE
WHAT TO DO, WHAT WOULD IT BE? MAKE YOUR CHOICES
BELOW. WHY NOT LET YOUR FRIENDS HAVE A GO, TOO,
AND SEE HOW YOUR ANSWERS COMPARE.

Would you rather ...

Chill out with Liam at his house, listening to One Direction CDs? 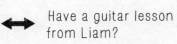 Have a guitar lesson from Liam?

Take Liam to meet your friends? 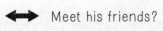 Meet his friends?

Go surfing with him? 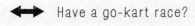 Have a go-kart race?

Walk along the beach together, collecting shells? 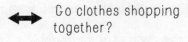 Go clothes shopping together?

Have fun at Disneyland? 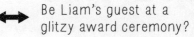 Be Liam's guest at a glitzy award ceremony?

Do backing vocals for a
new One Direction song? Appear as a dancer in a
1D music video?

Swim with dolphins
together? Go bungee jumping?

Be One Direction's
personal photographer? Be 1D's publicist?

Have Liam sing to you at
your birthday party? Have him cook a meal
for you at your home?

Go to the cinema
with Liam? Watch a DVD with
him at home?

Be Liam's BFF? Be the One Direction
tour manager?

Have a romantic
restaurant dinner
for two? Go for a fun meal with
Liam and your best
friends?

Have Liam write and
perform a song
all about you? Spend a day in a luxury
limo with him, travelling
around New York City?

All directions!

NO MATTER HOW YOU LOOK AT IT — UP, DOWN, ACROSS, BACK TO FRONT AND EVEN DIAGONALLY— EVERY WORD BELOW IS ASSOCIATED WITH LIAM. CAN YOU FIND THEM ALL? THE ANSWERS ARE ON **PAGE 94**.

LIAM PAYNE

NIALL

LOUIS

HARRY

ZAYN

SIMON COWELL

UP ALL NIGHT

ALL SAINTS

TAKE ME HOME

'GOTTA BE YOU'

TOY STORY

WOLVERHAMPTON

R	T	T	H	G	I	N	L	L	A	P	U	N	O	T
S	A	E	F	I	C	R	B	X	T	F	O	H	N	A
S	V	E	U	O	Y	E	B	A	T	T	O	G	E	K
E	H	N	E	O	E	A	L	M	P	S	C	V	T	E
T	O	Y	S	T	O	R	Y	M	B	H	L	T	G	M
A	O	A	M	N	V	H	A	Y	R	I	L	K	M	E
H	T	P	I	Z	R	H	C	I	O	U	E	C	E	H
B	T	M	K	E	R	H	S	D	Y	H	W	S	I	O
O	A	A	V	E	G	M	J	R	A	T	O	E	O	M
Y	T	I	V	T	Z	Q	R	S	N	K	C	L	D	E
K	E	L	E	N	I	A	L	L	C	G	N	Y	A	Z
W	O	D	T	J	H	T	O	D	E	N	O	A	B	I
W	F	I	I	T	D	U	N	L	H	I	M	E	D	A
I	N	S	H	G	I	H	N	Y	D	F	I	B	I	T
V	L	C	W	S	B	S	T	N	I	A	S	L	L	A

Fact-tastic!

ARE YOU TOP OF THE CLASS WHEN IT COMES TO KNOWING YOUR FACTS ABOUT LIAM? FIND OUT WITH THIS TEST. TICK THE BOXES NEXT TO THE FACTS YOU ALREADY KNEW. BE HONEST!

WHEN YOU ARE DONE, LOOK AT THE SUPER-FAN SCORECARD ON **PAGE 71** TO SEE HOW YOU HAVE FARED.

☐ Liam's nickname in the band is Daddy Direction.

☐ Liam got sunburnt feet in Barbados at Simon Cowell's house in 2008.

☐ Only one of Liam's kidneys functioned properly when he was a child and this is why he does not drink alcohol.

☐ Liam's dog, Brit, has a hoodie with a Union Jack flag and her name emblazoned on it.

☐ Liam has a phobia about spoons.

☐ He got his own back on a snooping press photographer in Sweden by throwing a snowball at him from his hotel balcony.

☐ Liam used to be a Scout.

☐ Liam and the One Direction boys were thrown out of a hotel swimming pool for 'dive-bombing' in just their boxer shorts.

☐ He is a self-taught guitarist and pianist.

☐ Liam would love to do a cover version of 'Hey Jude' by The Beatles.

☐ He considers himself to be the best dancer in One Direction.

☐ Liam says that he is the one who usually arranges the present whenever it's the birthday of one of his band mates. But none of the boys bother buying each other Christmas gifts.

SUPER-FAN SCORECARD   A+

Score 0–4
Must try harder. More commitment is necessary. You have a tendency for slackness and a lack of concentration.

Score 5–8
Shows promise. You try hard and are keen to progress but need to knuckle down to reach full potential.

Score 9–12
Well done! A fine performance. You have the dedication and enthusiasm to stay at the top of the class.

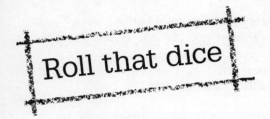

Roll that dice

DISCOVER YOUR DESTINY WITH LIAM. GRAB A DICE AND
FOLLOW THE INSTRUCTIONS BELOW.

1. Write your own idea in the 'Your choice' section for
each of the categories **A** to **E**.

2. Get rolling! Roll the dice once for each of the five
categories. The number you roll is the choice that the
dice has made for you.

3. Write down your future with Liam in the box on the
opposite page, and wait to see if it comes true.

CATEGORIES

A. Where you and Liam will meet:
1. Backstage at a concert **2.** In a restaurant **3.** Outside
a TV or recording studio **4.** At the airport **5.** In the
supermarket

6. (Your choice) ....

B. What you will do together:
1. Go to the zoo; **2.** Go on a hike; **3.** Sing a duet; **4.** Watch a
scary movie; **5.** Eat at a fancy restaurant

6. (Your choice) ....

C. What Liam will notice about you:
1. Your fashionable look **2.** Your brilliant sense of humour
3. Your gorgeous hair **4.** Your too-cool-for-school vibe
5. Your cheeky grin

6. (Your choice) ....

D. What he will give you as a gift:
1. A top-of-the-range phone **2.** A sports car **3.** Singing lessons **4.** Beautiful flowers every week **5.** A signed photo

6. (Your choice) ....

E. Where you and Liam will go:
1. Athens, Greece **2.** Sydney, Australia **3.** The Caribbean
4. New York, USA **5.** Kenya

6. (Your choice) ....

Your future with Liam:

I'm going to meet Liam ....

Together, we will ....

He'll be blown away by my ....

As a present, he will give me ....

We'll travel to ....

Timeline

HELP CHART LIAM'S ROAD TO STARDOM BY FILLING IN THE BLANKS ON HIS TIMELINE. THE MISSING WORDS ARE AT THE BOTTOM OF **PAGE 77**. INSERT THEM WHERE YOU THINK THEY SHOULD BE. THEN CHECK YOUR ANSWERS ON **PAGE 95**.

29th August 1993: Liam Payne is born in Wolverhampton, West Midlands.

2008: He has his first audition for *The X Factor* at the age of 14, singing .... (1). Cheryl Cole says, 'I like you. I think you're really cute. I think you've got charisma, you know, you give us that little cheeky wink.' Simon Cowell feels something is lacking, but Liam still goes through to the next round.

2008: At the judges' houses stage, Liam sings 'A Million Love Songs' in front of Simon Cowell and Sinitta. 'I'm afraid it's bad news,' says Simon, who tells Liam he is too young to go through and should concentrate on his GCSEs and come back in two years.

September 2009: Liam performs in front of a crowd of 29,000 at a Wolverhampton Wanderers football match against Manchester United.

2010: He returns to *The X Factor*, and sings ....

.... (2) and receives a standing ovation from the audience and Simon. 'Absolutely incredible,' says Simon. Liam sweeps through to the next round.

2010: At the bootcamp stage, he sings 'Stop Crying Your Heart Out'. Judge Louis Walsh tells Simon that he likes Liam. Simon replies, 'I like him. But I think he's a little bit one-dimensional.'

September 2010: In a surprising twist, Simon Cowell tells solo singers Liam, Zayn Malik, Louis Tomlinson, Niall Horan and Harry Styles that they are too good to let go and decides to put them into a group. Harry comes up with the name 'One Direction'. They perform at Simon's house in LA, singing Natalie Imbruglia's 'Torn'.

October 2010: In the first of the live shows, One Direction sing Coldplay's 'Viva la Vida' to much acclaim.

December 2010: One Direction perform with Robbie Williams, singing his hit song, '..

......................' (3), during *The X Factor* live final. They come third in the competition, losing out to winner Matt Cardle and runner-up Rebecca Ferguson.

March 2011: Liam proudly poses with the rest of the band as they release their first book *One Direction: Forever Young*, which climbs to the top of the bestseller list.

August 2011: Liam arrives at the Radio 1 London studios with his band mates for the first play of One Direction's debut single 'What Makes You Beautiful'.

September 2011: Their debut single reaches No. 1 in the UK Top 40. It goes on to spend 19 weeks in the charts.

February 2012: He flies to the USA with One Direction to begin a tour.

February 2012: One Direction win Best British Single at the Brit Awards. The boys beat nine other acts to scoop the prize for their debut track 'What Makes You Beautiful'.

March 2012: One Direction become the first British group to go straight to No. 1 in the US Billboard 200 chart with their album *Up All Night*.

April 2012: One Direction arrive in Sydney for their mini-tour of Australia and New Zealand.

May 2012: 'What Makes You Beautiful' goes double platinum in the US. The boys celebrate being one of the most successful British boy bands to make it in America.

August 2012: The One Direction boys perform 'What Makes You Beautiful' on a moving carnival float at the Olympics Closing Ceremony in London.

August 2012: One Direction announce that their second album will be called *Take Me Home*. The record's lead single, 'Live While We're Young', becomes the fastest selling pre-order song in history.

September 2012: One Direction win three MTV Video Music Awards. They beat Justin Bieber and ....

.... (4) in the Best Pop Video category for

'What Makes You Beautiful' and collect Best New Artist. The distinctive awards are astronaut figures, and taking to the stage to collect the second one, Harry says, 'To win one Moonman is amazing. To win two is incredible, and to perform is absolutely ridiculous. So thank you so much for having us.' After belting out 'One Thing', they pick up their third award for Most Share-Worthy Video.

November 2012: They release their second album *Take Me Home*.

November 2012: They do a UK chart double with their new single, 'Little Things', reaching No. 1 and their album *Take Me Home*, doing the same.

November 2012: 1D meet the Queen and perform at the .... (5) singing 'Little Things'.

December 2012: They play their biggest gig yet at New York's .... (6) in front of 20,000 screaming fans. Liam tells the crowd, 'This is just amazing.'

February 2013: One Direction embark on a world tour.

Missing words

Rihanna	Royal Variety Performance
'Fly Me To The Moon'	'She's The One'
Madison Square Garden	'Cry Me A River'

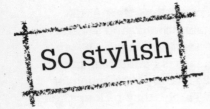

So stylish

FROM SWEET BOY-NEXT-DOOR TYPE TO THE HARD-MAN LOOK, LIAM DOESN'T MIND CHANGING AND EXPERIMENTING WITH HIS APPEARANCE.

READ ON TO FIND OUT MORE ABOUT LIAM'S STYLE CHOICES, THEN RATE HOW GORGEOUS YOU THINK HE LOOKS IN EACH OF THE OUTFITS DESCRIBED USING THE STYLE-O-METER BELOW.

Style-O-Meter

 Fashion Fail

 Could Do Better

Super Sweet

 Seriously Suave

 There Are No Words For How Hot He Looks!

Check it out
Liam loves checked shirts, particularly in a mix of red and blue. His wardrobe must be full of them!

Mr Bean
Like Harry, Liam is a big fan of beanie hats. Come to think of it, Harry and Liam must share each other's, as they both seem to have so many!

Hard man
Sweet, gentle, soft-haired, soft-faced Liam morphed into a hard man with buzz-cut hair and tight denims, plus no-nonsense grey round-necked T-shirts. It's certainly a macho look, but would you take this boy home to meet your mum?

In da hood
Liam loves a hoodie, and no one else can wear one and still look so angelic!

Superhero
He's always been into superheroes, and Batman is one of his favourites, so Liam jumped at the chance to dress as the caped crusader for a Halloween party in London. Did this superhero look super hot?

Bit of an animal
Louis says the 1D boys were startled when they noticed Liam's footwear while on the road. 'Liam once sat in the car and it took us 20 minutes before we looked down and noticed that he was wearing leopard-print shoes,' admits Louis. 'We were baffled!'

Hair today, gone tomorrow
Liam's ever-changing locks are a constant topic of conversation. His hair is Bieber-esque one moment and super-short the next. Liam explained that his long and curly style was the simplest to look after. 'What happened was, we went to a studio and I forgot my hair straighteners, and I didn't do anything and then I thought I can't be bothered straightening it again. I used to have to get up hours earlier to wash it, dry it, straighten it.' Why not go bald next, Liam? That would be even easier.

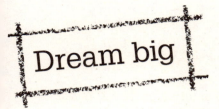

Dream big

LIAM DREAMED OF BEING A SINGER AND WAS DETERMINED TO GIVE IT HIS BEST SHOT. EVEN WHEN HE FAILED, HE GOT RIGHT BACK UP AND HAD ANOTHER GO.

READ SOME OF HIS INSPIRATIONAL AND MOTIVATIONAL QUOTES BELOW AND THEN ADD YOUR THOUGHTS AND ASPIRATIONS UNDERNEATH.

'Now I think Simon probably gave us the best advice, which was to be the band we wanna be, and I think that's great advice because it means we can keep it young, we can keep it fresh, you know, it's all good!'

What has been the best advice you have ever been given?

....
....
....
....
....
....
....

'A fortnight ago, I was just an ordinary lad from Wolverhampton, now there are screaming girls outside my window.'

Liam said this after his second audition on *The X Factor*. What do you think might be the disadvantage of being famous?

....

....

....

....

....

'The reason why I think I've got the X Factor is because I took a knock-back at an early age, I took on a huge challenge, set myself a goal and I never gave up.'

Liam impressed the *X Factor* judges when he said this for his second audition after failing to get through to the final two years earlier. Describe a time when you have got over a knock-back and had another go at something.

....

....

....

....

....

'I always told my dad I wanted to have everything I ever wanted by the time I was 21. That was my dream and I wanted to get there. I'm so lucky I'm on the way there and doing it with four of the best lads in the world.'

Which of your friends do you think you will know for the rest of your life?

....

....

....

'My family are so supportive of me and so proud.'

What or who always puts a smile on your face?

....

....

'That (winning three MTV Video Music Awards) and doing the Olympics was when I thought, this is bigger than I ever expected it to be.'

What has been the greatest achievement in your life so far?

....

....

....

'People had told me that I was a good singer so
I thought I would give it a go and audition for
The X Factor.'

What would you sing if you went on *The X Factor* and why?

....

....

....

....

....

'We all wanted to be soloists initially, so it was weird.
But I absolutely love being in the band. It was a tough
decision, but I'll never regret it, ever.'

**Liam described how strange the boys felt when they
were put together in a band. What has been the toughest
decision you have ever made?**

....

....

....

....

....

Headline news!

WHEN YOU ARE AS BIG AS ONE DIRECTION, EVERY LITTLE THING BECOMES HEADLINE NEWS. HERE ARE SOME OF THE MORE INTERESTING 1D HEADLINES. BUT NOT EVERYTHING IS AS IT SEEMS. SOME OF THE HEADLINES ARE REAL AND SOME ARE FAKE. CAN YOU SPOT WHICH ARE WHICH? THE ANSWERS ARE ON PAGE 95.

'LIAM'S HAIR TAKES NEW DIRECTION'

Liam's hair, it seems, has a mind of its own, and it's no surprise that everyone is looking out to see what style is next.

☐ True News ☐ Fake Fail

'I'LL QUIT TO GO SOLO'

He started off as a solo singer, of course, like each of his band mates, but does Liam really want to quit One Direction at some stage?

☐ True News ☐ Fake Fail

'LIAM PAYNE IS A SCROOGE'

Kind, generous, Liam? Bah humbug!

☐ True News ☐ Fake Fail

'IF IT HADN'T BEEN FOR ONE DIRECTION, I'D BE MAKING JET PARTS IN A FACTORY IN WOLVERHAMPTON'

Well, we're sure that's a good, worthwhile and satisfying job, Liam. But did he actually say it?

☐ True News   ☐ Fake Fail

'MY GOOD-NESS! WAS THAT A MONSTER?'

While on holiday in the Highlands of Scotland as a child, Liam saw a mysterious shape on Loch Ness and he thinks it may have been the legendary Loch Ness Monster.

☐ True News   ☐ Fake Fail

'WHAT DIRECTION WAS THAT?'

Liam got hopelessly lost in his car when he made a mess of the directions.

☐ True News   ☐ Fake Fail

'JUST GIVE ME FINGER FOOD'

Liam told how his phobia about spoons had spread to knives and forks.

☐ True News   ☐ Fake Fail

'DOCTOR PAYNE'

As a schoolboy he considered the medical profession as a possible career, but his dad said that 'Dr Payne' might not be very comforting for his patients!

☐ True News   ☐ Fake Fail

'ONE DIRECTION'S LIAM PAYNE CATCHES SHARK DURING FISHING TRIP'

Liam reeled in a big one during a fishing trip in California.

☐ True News   ☐ Fake Fail

'ONE DIRECTION STAR LIAM PAYNE HAS BROKEN HIS TOE'

He felt all footloose after dropping a lap-top on his toe, which gave him the kind of break he could do without.

☐ True News   ☐ Fake Fail

'LIAM'S UNDIE-WHELMED!'

During One Direction's gig at Madison Square Garden in New York, a fan threw a pair of undies at him with Liam's picture on the front of them!

☐ True News   ☐ Fake Fail

'CAUGHT WITH HIS PANTS UP'

Well, it's different! Liam pulled up a pair of undies on TV in Australia.

☐ True News   ☐ Fake Fail

LIAM IS LUSH

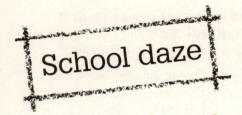

School daze

THE HEAD TEACHER OF YOUR SCHOOL HAS ANNOUNCED THAT A CELEBRITY IS VISITING ON THE LAST DAY OF TERM. BUT THE IDENTITY OF THE STAR IS SECRET ...

This is only the beginning of the story. Now it's up to you to develop it by filling in the gaps below. You can use the ideas in brackets to help you, or simply make it up as you go along.

All the pupils wonder who the mystery celebrity will be. Nobody famous has ever attended your school. So who could it be?

One girl suggests it might be ...Liam................... ,
but another hopes it will be ...Niall................... .
But you don't think it will be anyone as famous as that.

The morning of the big day arrives, and all the pupils are talking excitedly on the way to school about the star's arrival. It's going to be really hard concentrating in lessons.

As the morning assembly draws to an end, the Head announces from the stage, 'And now, it's the moment that I know you have all been waiting for. I'd like to introduce our special visitor this morning. But before I do, I thought I might give you some clues.' Everyone groans. This is agonizing. Get on with it! There's only one person you really want it to be, and it's certainly not going to be him.

'He's a singer,' says the Head, 'and part of one of the biggest bands in the world.' The excitement reaches fever pitch. But you are sure the Head is exaggerating. It's probably someone you have barely heard of.

The Head turns to the side of the stage, smiles and says, 'Come on out.'

To your jaw-dropping amazement, it's your idol, Liam Payne!

You can't believe your eyes and turn to your friends and comment: 'Am i dreaming '
(Am I dreaming?/ I can't believe this!/ He's quite a good Liam look-alike, isn't he?)

Liam walks over to the mic and with a huge smile on his face says: ' Hi, I'm Liam '
(Hi, I'm Liam./ Are you having a nice morning?/ I'd like to thank the Head for inviting me.)

When the screams have died down, Liam says he wanted to come to your school because one of his cousins used to be a pupil here .
(One of the pupils had written to ask him/ He chose it at random/ One of his cousins used to be a pupil there)

Liam then asks if anyone would like to fire a question at him. Lots of hands shoot up but, to your amazement, he points at you and asks your name.

You reply: ' My name is Emma c '

'And what would you like to ask me?' he says with a warm smile.

You ask: 'Will you marry me ?'
(Will you marry me?/ Would you help me with my homework?/ Do you get paid well being a Liam Payne look-alike?)

Liam laughs and replies: 'no not yet .'

And you say: 'OK .'

After others get to ask questions, the Head says it's time to go to your lessons, while Liam looks around the school. Not surprisingly, it's hard to focus on studies, and there's a lot of whispering going on. Everyone keeps looking at the door, hoping that Liam will walk in. But he doesn't.

At lunchtime, you join the food queue. Suddenly, you see the Head walk in with Liam. The Head tells everyone to calm down and carry on with what they are doing, but you are surprised when Liam takes his place in the queue right behind you! You turn and both smile at each other.

Liam says: 'Fancy meeting you again .'
(You made me laugh at assembly./ Fancy meeting you again./ What's the food like here?)

You tell him that the best thing to eat here is: 'f .'

Liam says that he will give it a try.

Everyone's watching you enviously, but Liam is focusing on you alone. He asks if he can sit down with you to eat.

The Head has reserved an empty table for Liam, but Liam asks if you could join him along with some of your friends. The Head replies, 'Of course. In fact, I'll leave you to chat with the pupils. I'm sure they don't want me around.' Bliss!

Liam asks the names of your best friends at school and you tell him .... and ....

and .... and ....

When you sit down, you call for your friends to join you. Liam tells you all about being in One Direction and how great the band's fans are. You tell him that you are a huge fan – especially of him. He laughs and says:

'..,'

(Would you like my autograph?/ How about some tickets for you and your friends to our next gig?/ Maybe I should bring the rest of the band here soon and we could do a special gig on the school stage.)

You reply: '.. .'

After he has finished his food, Liam gets up and says he has to go and join his band mates for a rehearsal but that he has had a lovely time at your school.

He gives you a hug and then gives you: ....

....

(his phone number/ a backstage pass to his next gig/ his hat to keep as a memento)

'Until next time,' he says with a smile, and off he goes.

What a day this has been. If only school days were always like this!

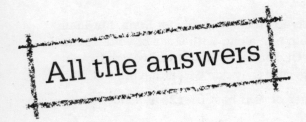

All the answers

Forever young
Pages 10–12

1.	a	**6.**	b	**11.**	b
2.	b	**7.**	b	**12.**	a
3.	a	**8.**	a	**13.**	c
4.	c	**9.**	a	**14.**	b
5.	a	**10.**	c		

Cringe!
Pages 14–15

1.	True Cringe	**4.**	Fake Fail	**7.**	Fake Fail
2.	True Cringe	**5.**	True Cringe		
3.	True Cringe	**6.**	Fake Fail		

Super-fans
Pages 16–18

1.	True Tale	**6.**	True Tale	**11.**	True Tale
2.	Fan Fake	**7.**	Fan Fake	**12.**	Fan Fake
3.	Fan Fake	**8.**	True Tale	**13.**	Fan Fake
4.	True Tale	**9.**	Fan Fake	**14.**	Fan Fake
5.	True Tale	**10.**	True Tale		

Hot favourites
Pages 25–27

1.	c	**4.**	b	**7.**	c	**10.**	b	**13.**	b
2.	b	**5.**	a	**8.**	a	**11.**	a		
3.	a	**6.**	a	**9.**	a	**12.**	c		

True or false?
Pages 28–29

1. True
2. False – it was Louis.
3. True
4. False – it was Niall.
5. False – it was Harry.

6. True
7. True
8. True
9. True
10. False – it was Zayn.

What was the question?
Pages 32–33

1. F
2. G
3. B
4. A
5. D

Guess who?
Pages 44–45

1. Zayn
2. The name of his first child
3. His sisters
4. Jay-Z
5. Niall
6. Zayn
7. 'Live While We're Young'

Spot the difference
In the picture section

1. The white pattern has been taken off Liam's shirt sleeve.
2. A black button has been added to Louis's shirt.
3. Niall has two red wristbands.
4. Harry's shoes have been changed to blue.
5. Harry's hanky is now red.
6. The blonde has been removed from Zayn's hair.
7. Zayn's coat sleeve is blue.
8. Zayn's no longer has a watch on.

All directions!
Pages 68–69

R	T	T	H	C	I	N	L	L	A	P	U	N	O	T
S	A	E	F	I	C	R	B	X	T	F	O	H	N	A
S	V	E	U	O	Y	E	B	A	T	T	O	C	E	K
E	H	N	E	O	E	A	L	M	P	S	C	V	T	E
T	O	Y	S	T	O	R	Y	M	B	H	L	T	C	M
A	O	A	M	N	V	H	A	Y	R	I	L	K	M	E
H	T	P	I	Z	R	C	I	O	U	E	C	E	H
B	T	M	K	E	R	H	S	D	Y	H	W	S	I	O
O	A	A	V	C	M	J	R	A	T	O	E	O	M
Y	T	V	T	Z	Q	R	S	N	K	C	L	D	E
K	E	L	E	N	I	A	L	L	C	C	N	Y	A	Z
W	O	D	T	J	H	T	O	D	E	N	O	A	B	I
W	F	I	I	T	D	U	N	L	H	I	M	E	D	A
I	N	S	H	C	I	H	N	Y	D	F	B	I	T
V	L	C	W	S	B	S	T	N	I	A	C	L	L	A

Timeline
Pages 74–77

1. 'Fly Me To The Moon'
2. 'Cry Me A River'
3. 'She's The One'
4. Rihanna
5. Royal Variety Performance
6. Madison Square Garden

Headline news!
Pages 85–87

'LIAM'S HAIR TAKES NEW DIRECTION' – True News

'I'LL QUIT TO GO SOLO' – Fake Fail

'LIAM PAYNE IS A SCROOGE' – True News

'IF IT HADN'T BEEN FOR ONE DIRECTION, I'D BE
MAKING JET PARTS IN A FACTORY IN WOLVERHAMPTON'
– True News

'MY GOOD-NESS! WAS THAT A MONSTER?' – Fake Fail

'WHAT DIRECTION WAS THAT?' – Fake Fail

'JUST GIVE ME FINGER FOOD' – Fake Fail

'DOCTOR PAYNE' – Fake Fail

'ONE DIRECTION'S LIAM PAYNE CATCHES SHARK DURING
FISHING TRIP' – True News

'ONE DIRECTION STAR LIAM PAYNE HAS BROKEN
HIS TOE' – True News

'LIAM'S UNDIE-WHELMED!' – Fake Fail

'CAUGHT WITH HIS PANTS UP' – True News